PREPARING YOUR CATHOLIC WEDDING

Preparing Your Catholic Wedding

Practical Considerations

T. JEROME OVERBECK, SJ
with
Rudy T. Marcozzi

ALBA·HOUSE NEW·YORK
SOCIETY OF ST. PAUL, 2187 VICTORY BLVD., STATEN ISLAND, NEW YORK 10314

ST PAULS

Library of Congress Cataloging-in-Publication Data

Overbeck, T. Jerome.
Preparing your Catholic wedding: practical considerations / T. Jerome Overbeck with Rudy T. Marcozzi.
p. cm.
Includes bibliographical references.
ISBN 0-8189-0904-8 (alk. paper)
1. Marriage—Religious aspects—Catholic Church. 2. Wedding etiquette. 3. Marriage service. 4. Catholic Church—Liturgy—Texts. I. Marcozzi, Rudy T. (Rudy Thomas) II. Title.

BX2250.O94 2002
264'.02085—dc21

2001055324

Imprimi Potest:
Richard J. Baumann, SJ
Provincial, Chicago Province
October 16, 2001

Produced and designed in the United States of America by the Fathers and Brothers of the Society of St. Paul, 2187 Victory Boulevard, Staten Island, New York 10314-6603, as part of their communications apostolate.

ISBN: 0-8189-0904-8

Printing Information:

Current Printing - first digit 1 2 3 4 5 6 7 8 9 10

Year of Current Printing - first year shown

2002 2003 2004 2005 2006 2007 2008 2009 2010

Preface

This book is primarily for a bride and groom planning a Catholic wedding. For twenty-five years I have helped hundreds of couples like yourselves celebrate their weddings. Reflecting upon these experiences has given me a unique perspective. Since I have found that many of the same issues recur with great frequency, I wanted to provide those approaching their wedding trail with some guideposts set by those who have gone before you. *— T. Jerome Overbeck, SJ*

As a church musician, I have been privileged to coordinate and perform the music for countless wedding liturgies. Celebrating a wedding liturgy that is both prayerful and festive is no small feat, but in the course of a twelve-year collaboration, I have watched Fr. Overbeck help couples do this time and time again in astonishingly different situations. His pastoral sensitivity, attention to detail, and warm presidential style are superb gifts to the church, and are evident in the wise counsel he provides in this book. I was delighted to contribute the chapter on music and act as his general editor. *— Rudy T. Marcozzi*

In each chapter, we use a short story related from our experiences as an entry point into the information that follows.

We have been intentionally brief so that your reading will not become an onerous burden in the midst of your many preparations. Summary points follow each chapter for easy reference. We hope that our efforts will allow you to tell your story through an engaging, joyous, and prayerful wedding liturgy.

AMDG
Chicago, IL 2001

Table of Contents

Chapter 1: Whose Wedding Is It, Anyway? 1

Chapter 2: If We Can Survive This Wedding... 13

Chapter 3: Paperwork Drives Me Nuts 19

Chapter 4: Options 27

Chapter 5: What About the Music? 57

Chapter 6: The High Cost of Marrying 69

Appendix A: Recipes for Eucharistic Bread 73

Appendix B: More Resources for Music 75

PREPARING YOUR CATHOLIC WEDDING

Chapter One

Whose Wedding Is It, Anyway?

> With the best of intentions, the groom seemed ever-so-gracious in volunteering his perspective on their approaching marriage: "It's her (the bride's) wedding—whatever she wants is fine with me."

So whose wedding is it? The bride's? The mother of the bride's? The mother of the groom's? The priest's? The one paying the bills? The photographer's? The wedding consultant's? What significant factors determine whose wedding it is? Does all this matter, or is it much ado about nothing?

In fact, it matters tremendously. The look and feel of your wedding ceremony depends upon how you, operationally, answer this question: whose wedding is it? If you have never been a bride or groom before, you have never faced preparing *your* marriage. Couples like you know only as much as you have experienced through the weddings of a few others. While most educated brides and grooms like yourselves have read many books, few if any of you have explored the kinds of issues and concerns you are likely to face when planning your marriage ceremony.

Whose wedding is it? We can take a cue from the centuries-old understanding of the faith community.[1] The minister of the marriage is not the priest. The bride ministers the sacrament to the groom; the groom ministers the sacrament to the bride. The bride and groom celebrate the covenant. Those who gather for your wedding along with the presiding priest, in their own name and in the name of all the Church, pray that God will bless your lifelong commitment of love.

Whose wedding is it? Recently a photographer quipped: "Don't kid yourself—the marriage is for the bride and groom, but the wedding is for the mother of the bride." Some think it is a laudable ideal to educate you as a marrying couple in such a way that you become capable of taking more and more responsibility for your own sacrament and how it is celebrated. Others, like the photographer quoted above, think it is not realistic to build such expectations (even through education) because, in the end, the mother of the bride will call all the shots—a rather cynical view in my opinion. Seeing the reality of your wedding without hope of educating you toward freer and more careful decisions does not seem particularly Christian.

First of all, not every mother of the bride is a clone of some narrow-minded authoritarian. If we are to monitor our own prejudices, we need to remember that each person is an individual. Some, for the sake of their son or daughter, respond in ways their children do not expect—sometimes in ways which help; at other times in ways which complicate matters. This is what we have found to be the best approach: explore the details of the ceremony with your priest presider, apart from anyone else, including the mother of the bride.

By now you, as bride and groom, should see that the best answer to "Whose wedding is it?" is "It's *our* wedding." But even if you believe this and have come to own this answer, having it actually shape your wedding ceremony will be no small task. Begin with the person you have chosen as your presider. You especially need your priest to see and understand the value of your style of wedding. The American bishops stated that the attitude, style and bearing of the presider affect the liturgy more than any other single factor.[2] You need your presider to be "on board."

In order to protect your primary role as the bride and groom in the wedding, sit down with the priest (and no one else) about six months before the ceremony. You need this amount of time to prepare carefully for your sacrament and not to feel rushed. Ask your presider to help you in these *five ways*:

1. Remember, it's your wedding, not the presider's. To help your presider get a clear understanding of what you want, you must clarify that understanding for yourselves. This clarifying may take some time for thought, conversation and prayer for you to discern what each of you really wants. It will take effort on your part to figure this out for yourselves. And you must do this before you attempt to tell anyone else. One way to proceed that might help: take a little time to do some private soul-searching on your own. Ask yourself individually: "Of all the facets of our relationship which I could point to and identify in the light of God's Word during our wedding ceremony, what two or three simple statements (sentences) could I set down for the presider and preacher to emphasize?" Then talk with each other about the statements you formulated. Chances are there will be some overlap between you. You might prefer the way your partner has expressed it because, now that you think about it, he or she says it better, in a more significant way. You might want to combine a few statements. When the two of you have decided on what you want to emphasize in the celebration of your life together, bring the list to the presider (and to the preacher, if he is different from the presider). This will help you tailor the

wedding to the two of you and *your* family and friends and will make it feel less like a "generic" wedding.

2. Ask the priest to help you identify and collect the paper work which the Catholic Church and the State require of every marrying couple.
3. Request some material from him to read, so you can learn a little more about the significance of the step you are about to take and the process of celebrating your marriage in a meaningful way.
4. Ask if he will lead the rehearsal of your wedding ceremony and come join you at the rehearsal dinner. Do not underestimate how this helps the presider and preacher personalize the ceremony and make it less generic.
5. Of course, be sure he will preside at the wedding itself, and invite him to the reception. If he will take the time and invest the energy, the reception is fertile ground for fun, conversation, reflection, and further communion.

Do not assume that all priests will help in these five ways. With the current shortage of priests, some are over-worked and will not be able to. Others will not care to offer all of these services. Ask. Do not presume the services he will provide. If the priest declines, you decide if you want to go elsewhere and ask another priest. Again, be careful not to presume that your assumptions are his.

In your planning for your wedding, explicitly INSIST THAT THE PRIEST TAKE THE LEAD AT THE REHEARSAL. Ask him not to allow anyone else to re-work the ceremony at the rehearsal. Not the wedding coordinator. Not the mothers of the bride and groom. No one.

At the rehearsal, ask the priest to describe each portion of the wedding ceremony in detail, *as the bride and groom want to celebrate it.* While leading the rehearsal, the priest will need to listen attentively for any well-intentioned comment within earshot like: "Well, that's nice, but I saw a wedding once where they..." (and they describe some variation which the bride and groom chose to exclude). In your meetings with the priest to prepare your wedding, indicate to him that if this happens, he should literally step between the one asking the question and you (the bride or groom) who might be tempted to answer. Ask him to respond, quickly expressing some gratitude for their suggestion, but also adding that the bride and groom and he have been meeting for many months weighing possibilities (like this suggestion), and the bride and groom have decided to ask us to do it this way... "So, could the maid of honor stand here..." (and let the priest just keep talking). If the one who offered the idea gets in a tizzy, the person will probably be angry with the priest for a little while because he railroaded an approach different from theirs. But, at least you, as the primary actors in this wedding, will be protected from this "no win" situation. If you simply acquiesce and go along with their suggestion, you will almost certainly feel: "Damn it, I cannot even have my own wedding the way I want it."

If you choose to speak up and reject their suggestion yourself instead of letting the priest do it for you, you had better be ready for the emotional displeasure of parents or friends who may get in a royal snit over the whole matter. You don't need that kind of disturbance the evening before your wedding. There is enough pressure without added misunderstanding. And you must realize, too, that if you entertain a new suggestion at the rehearsal itself, then it becomes "open season" for anyone to ask you to reconsider any other part of the wedding which was supposed to be yours. Let the priest answer the person making the suggestion with whatever you as bride and groom and he as priest have prepared.

Even though it is your wedding, you minister the sacrament

to each other in a public ritual. The prayer is not private and exclusively individual, but public and inclusively common. The common element involves more than just the two of you as bride and groom, for you come from a network of relationships. If you do not consider the thoughts and feelings of others who care deeply about you and your marriage, you may find yourselves knee-deep in emotionally-charged animosity for years to come, maybe a lifetime.

Listen with care to the perspectives of others *before* you finalize your plans. As bride and groom you would do well to refrain from deciding quickly on any specific issue. Wait until you take some time apart to think, talk, and pray through others' insights and suggestions. Otherwise the wheel which squeaks the loudest may end up getting the most grease. Operating in this "squeaky-wheel" mode can produce decisions which may extinguish an immediate brush fire of engulfing emotions but also result in long-lasting regrets—a wedding which has become a hodge-podge of your ideas and those of others, but with little integrity.

As bride and groom, you can respond to the suggestions of others in a variety of ways. For example, if it were my wedding, whether each place-setting for dinner had *favors* (those little decorative packages of candies or nuts) or not is just not something I would invest money, time and energy to consider. Recently I heard a couple lamenting the fact that they had responded poorly to Aunt Mary's query: "Who is bringing the favors?" The groom deftly retorted: "Oh, we're not going to mess with things like that... there won't be any at the reception." At which point, Aunt Mary became almost hysterical—fainting, sobs, the works. Was it worth the explosion? Could it have been forestalled? Perhaps if enough questions had been asked ahead of time, the couple might have defused this land mine by uncovering some of the layered significance that Aunt Mary had associated with favors over the lifetime of the bride. For instance, the bride and groom might have responded to the aunt's question something like this:

> "Aunt Mary, why did you ask about the favors? Help me understand what they mean to you."

Then follow your question and Aunt Mary's response with a comment like:

> "Let us give your suggestion some thought and prayer. We will talk about it and get back to you. Okay? Thanks a million for offering your help."

One can pray about the sublime and the ridiculous, even party favors. Reflect upon any suggestion in light of the Gospel. For example, ask yourself: "What would Jesus do in this situation?" In the end, if you decide upon something different from what the person has offered, you could suggest another way in which the person might be of assistance. It gives them an opportunity to lend you a hand and to participate, to feel included. Reasonable people will be pleased to help out in some way, even if their particular preference is by-passed and they feel some initial sting.

But remember, not everyone is reasonable. Since we each peer at the world through our own eyes, one person's meddling can be seen by another as helpful care. Be aware that some people offer to help with strings attached; while others are clearer that the primary point is meeting your needs as the marrying couple and not their own. Preparing any wedding, including yours, is messy business. When individuals are sincere, that is, they do not *intend* to complicate your life and make it more difficult, it can hurt all the more.

Most of the time church personnel are helpful. They recognize that they are there to serve you and the whole community. However, sometimes parish staff members, including priests, are unreasonable. (Not too surprising, since we are all human, a mixed bag.) For example, you may run into a situation where the priest at the church in which you imagine celebrating your wedding seems to take his cues from Seinfeld's "Soup Nazi" (a "my way or the highway" type). A steamrolling priest may demand that you celebrate your wedding *his way*—by using kneelers, for instance. He may issue edicts like "You *must* use kneelers for a Catholic wedding!" If this demand or some other is not something you want in *your* wedding, and yet you are not sure if in fact this is required in Catholicism throughout the world, you might want to consult another knowledgeable and wise Church leader.

Usually it does make sense to celebrate your sacrament in the context of the community in which you worship on Sundays. However, sometimes there are good reasons for an exception. As the American Bishops' Committee on the Liturgy reminded us decades ago, rubrics (rules) are not for their own sake, to be followed slavishly.[3]

This may be the first time you have ever dealt directly with the church staff about something you need. Understandably you might be a bit hesitant, perhaps a little intimidated. Most of the time, the parish staff is cordial and helpful. Once in a while, you will bump into some whose services you need for your wedding and whose demands are unreasonable. Occasionally these people are in positions to make a decision which could affect your wedding significantly. They could be the receptionist, the parish wedding coordinator, the musician, the florist, etc.

Sometimes people run "their parish" as if it were "their dukedom," and their orthodoxy police enforce the rule: "It has always been done this way in *real* Catholic weddings." Yes, the

Catholic Church needs some order; and, yes, knowledge of history and theology can liberate narrow rigidity. But the truth of the matter is that wedding customs have diversified considerably in the last twenty-five to thirty years. Usually I recommend that brides and grooms read the chapter on marriage in *From Beginning to End: The Rituals of Our Lives.*[4] There is no substitute for knowledge concerning the origins of many wedding customs. The way some people talk, you would think a particular way of celebrating a wedding goes back to the Garden of Eden or some immutable sacred place and time. You would do well to *think* about how you choose to proceed and why. Be careful to safeguard choices which rightly belong to you, the bride and groom.

Look carefully at a wide spectrum of alternatives. As bride and groom, try on each alternative for size, and ask yourself: "Is this for us?" In the end, if you each choose the same alternative as one that you witnessed at the wedding of your sister or friend, that's fine. At least you are deciding from a freer perspective, having scanned a range of options, imagined other possibilities, and are choosing with fewer blinders (which eliminate even seeing alternatives). What many marrying couples find in playing with alternatives is that they never knew there were so many ways to celebrate their wedding. Some make more sense than others for a particular couple, in a particular gathering of family and friends, at a particular time and place. This is one of the most important events in one's lifetime. For a Catholic, it is one of the seven most important forms of common prayer (sacraments). The way you prepare for your wedding deserves careful thought and prayer. "Winging it" is not an intelligent option for you as an educated bride and groom.

Be careful with the wedding consultant or coordinator. Sometimes they forget that you are paying them to work *for you.* This wedding is not theirs. I have witnessed many coordinators who will tell you, the bride and groom, the "right way" to celebrate your wedding. From what they say, you would think there is no deviating from their approach, even if you want to do so. Their non-verbal body language can communicate a charged message: "Go ahead if you want, but remember, I told you so. This is my business, but if you want to be the laughing stock of the city, it's up to you!"

You could easily become overwhelmed at the prospect of preparing your own wedding or assume that your experience reveals all that is possible. Often couples are unaware that they do not even know enough to formulate the right questions, let alone reach the right answers, establish priorities, and choose ways to proceed which make good sense. Sometimes couples bounce back and forth between feeling overwhelmed and being overconfident that "things are under control." Frequently couples find themselves moving quickly from an initial euphoria at the public announcement that "we're engaged" to an ever-growing maelstrom of questions which blind-side them.

It takes more than meets the eye to prepare your wedding so that it becomes one of the most wonderful events in your lives. Even if each of you has deep faith and proceeds carefully, it is likely that you will step on an emotional land mine periodically. Take heart. Others before you have survived.

Summary Points:

* The answer to the question "Whose wedding is it?" will shape and define your wedding ceremony.
* The Catholic response to this question is: "It is the wedding of the bride and groom." The bride ministers the sacrament to the groom; the groom ministers the sacrament to the bride.

* Work with your presider to clarify and define a ceremony that will truly be yours. Allow him to implement and realize your vision at the rehearsal and ceremony.
* While it is your wedding, it is everyone's prayer. Consider a broad variety of suggestions from those around you. Involve them constructively before you make any final decisions.
* Avoid hasty and unthoughtful snap-judgments. Allow yourself time to think and pray. Read for a better understanding of the possibilities that are open to you.

Notes

[1] Joseph J. Koury, S.J., "Marriage, Canonical Issues Concerning" in *The New Dictionary of Sacramental Worship* (Collegeville, MN: The Liturgical Press, 1990), pp. 776-789.

[2] American Bishops' Committee on the Liturgy, *Music In Catholic Worship* (Washington, DC: United States Catholic Conference, 1972), number 21.

[3] "No set of rubrics or regulations of itself will ever achieve a truly pastoral celebration of the sacramental rites. Such regulations must always be applied with a pastoral concern for the given worshiping community." American Bishops' Committee on the Liturgy, *Music In Catholic Worship* (Washington, DC: National Conference of Catholic Bishops, 1972), number 41.

[4] Robert Fulghum, *From Beginning to End: The Rituals of Our Lives* (New York: Ballantine Books, 1996), pp. 117-160.

Chapter Two

If We Can Survive This Wedding...

Chagrined over yet another blow-up with one of the women in their wedding party, the bride blurted out to the groom: "The sooner we get this thing (the wedding) over, the better. We are great together. It's all these crazy interactions around the wedding. Maybe we should elope! Oh well, once things get back to 'normal' we'll be fine."

The intensity and volume of preparations for a wedding come in waves. Generally the first month or two after the public announcement of your engagement can be exceptionally busy. Once you take care of these initial relatively simple tasks, get ready for other busy periods when the intensity and the volume will pick up again, especially closer to the actual wedding date. Then you'll look back and realize how easy the previous time really was.

Depending upon when you read this, it may seem ludicrous to present a chapter on "survival." Survival should be a "given," like the flag, mother, and apple pie. The goal of your wedding or its preparation should not be mere survival. Thriving is the goal—not surviving. Survival mode settles for the bare minimum. This hardly seems appropriate as a frame of mind and heart for celebrating what matters most in your lives, namely, your love for each other. Something is radically wrong if survival mode becomes your usual way of operating.

One piece of advice: the closer you come to the date of your wedding (within a year), take a certain amount of time "off the top." Reserve it for the two of you. You decide how much time—a few hours every ten days, one night every week, an extended lunch every other week. The amount of time is less crucial than its regularity and its quality. Just reserve regular quality time on your calendars, weeks and months ahead, for the two of you to do something fun together—absolutely nothing related to the wedding. This time is not for running wedding errands. This time is not to formulate strategies for dealing with someone in the wedding party whose relationship is becoming problematic. It is time "off the top" for the two of you to just *be* together, to enjoy one another's company, to rekindle your sense of why you wanted to do this wedding in the first place. Go jog together, have a picnic, go to a carnival or a street fair, amble through the countryside, rent a movie, go out to dinner.

Tell no one about this time. Others may get upset if they are working on some aspect of your wedding celebration and they know the two of you are off enjoying some break time. When someone attempts to lure you away from this time, say something like:

> "Oh, I'd like to do that with you, but my fiance and I have a prior commitment regarding the wedding. It involves several peoples' schedules, and there is no way to change them at this point. Maybe another time."

No one has a right to demand an explanation for the way you choose to spend your time. They can ask and you can decline. They have no right to demand. If they do, tell them it is none of their business.

If family and friends have offered to help and they choose to work at addressing invitations, for example, during the same hours you have set aside for the two of you to simply enjoy the evening, do not let yourself be manipulated by them or by your own unhealthy guilt. You can sabotage your own wedding without intending to do so. Do not forego your evening alone together by falling back into more chores related to the wedding. As a couple, you need a critical mass of quality "down time" on a regular basis. This is not a luxury, though it may seem so at the time.

Take care of yourselves. Without adequate time for rest and fun together, you can expect to arrive at the wedding emotionally bankrupt, just wanting to "get the damn thing over with." What a disheartening frame of mind to bring to the celebration of Christian love with a group of people who will never gather again under the same roof for this purpose. To have invested yourselves and a considerable amount of time, money and energy in months of preparation, and then to experience little joy in the wedding that you planned makes no sense.

Surely you have noticed that it is easy to make stupid decisions with the best of intentions. Hindsight often reveals how short-sighted we can sometimes be. Many married couples have expressed their gratitude for having been alerted to the need for reserving such quality time together *while in the midst of planning their wedding*. They inevitably say something like:

> "Thanks for the sound advice about taking regular quality time together for fun, especially the closer we got to the wedding. We took your advice, but it was so tempting to think that there were other things that were more urgent. We would kid ourselves repeat-

edly into imagining that we were alright... and then put our individual needs and our needs as a couple 'on hold.' In time this would take its toll. If anything, I would recommend you advise other couples approaching their wedding to take more time 'off the top,' not less. Encourage, even challenge them to protect the time for themselves as individuals and as a couple from everything else with which they might be tempted to replace it."

A final note about thriving as a goal. Money does not need to be a major factor in reserving regular quality time for each other. It costs nothing to take a walk in a park. Find a quiet place to cuddle while listening to your favorite kind of music. You can be creative in finding ways to inspire (the word means "breathe new life into") each other. Regularly invest some time to recognize that you are in the presence of God. Again, take time to be with people, places and things which tend to re-create you.

It is all too easy to let yourselves be overwhelmed by all the details involved in planning for your wedding. Without recognizing it, you can become so totally absorbed in making plans for the big day that you risk "burn out." Instead, it would be better to have fewer amenities and arrive at your day with more of you intact, with a sense of peace and joy, truly ready to celebrate who and what matters most to you. Forget the nonsense that you have to cross every *t* and dot every *i* if it means physical and emotional exhaustion and psychological and spiritual fragmentation. While the wedding may look good on the outside (to everyone else), the inner cost (to you, the bride and groom) could be substantial. In contrast to popular thinking, "looking good" is never the ultimate goal of a Christian. God does not judge by appearances.[1] *Being* good inside far surpasses "looking good" on the surface.

Obviously, you need to be careful about the amount and quality of time, energy, and money you invest in externals. But if you neglect your inner lives as individuals and as a couple, your spirits will eventually wane and perhaps even die. You will find yourselves going through the motions of your rehearsal, wedding and reception just trying to get it over with. In order not to slip passively into survival mode, make choices which enable you to thrive as a couple and as individuals.

Summary Points:

* Thriving is the goal—not surviving.
* Weeks and months ahead of the wedding, schedule regular quality time for you to do nothing together.
* Do not let yourself be manipulated by others or by your own unhealthy guilt. You can sabotage your own wedding without intending to do so.
* It's easy to let yourselves be overwhelmed, consumed and totally absorbed with planning all the details of your wedding.
* "Looking good" may be the popular goal, but this should never be the ultimate goal of a Christian.
* Neglecting your inner lives as individuals and as a couple will cause your spirits to wane. You will find yourselves going through the motions with little joy or enthusiasm.

Notes

[1] 1 Samuel 16:7.

Chapter Three

Paperwork Drives Me Nuts

The groom rolled his eyes and blurted out: "Rules, rules, rules!... What is the point of all this paperwork? Why can't we just get married and forget all the forms!"

Like it or not, paperwork is part of getting married. Before people do anything of significance in this culture—buy a car, go to school, rent an apartment, purchase insurance—they need to complete forms and sign on the dotted line. In significant matters, as the principal adult players, you are supposed to know what you're committing yourselves to, and be clear that if you miss a payment, the organization will take back the major item you thought was yours and they may well come after you as well. This is not a game. It is serious business. The same is true for marriage.

There are two kinds of paperwork: (1) paperwork for the State, and (2) paperwork for the Church.

The State requires that you have a valid marriage license. You can only obtain one within a specified number of days before the date of your wedding. For example in Cook County, Illinois, the license is valid for sixty days after the date of issuance. Some other counties have different lengths of time. You must be sure to have this State marriage license *from the county in which you will celebrate your marriage*. In some areas of the country this is no small matter, since multiple counties may be close together. The bride may live in one county, the groom in another, and the church for the wedding will be in still another. The priest cannot proceed with the wedding if you do not have a valid State license issued by the correct county.

Although this sounds obvious, remember the location of the "safe place" you put the license. At the very latest, by the time of the wedding rehearsal the priest needs the State marriage license *from the county of the church where you will wed.*

You may find the whole business of scheduling unpleasant because you need to consider many peoples' schedules in addition to your own. Usually the parish church serves thousands of people. You need the church personnel to schedule your wedding *and your rehearsal* in conjunction with the reservations of the place for your wedding reception and rehearsal dinner. In scheduling these times and places, you need to consider those whom you hope will attend your wedding and rehearsal. For example besides your schedules, you may want to consult each of your families, the wedding party, the priest who you hope will preside, etc. A common occurrence is that a bride and groom schedule the reception hall and assume the church is available. Proceeding in this manner can become a real nightmare. Churches and reception halls are often booked up to a year or more in advance, especially during late Spring and early Fall. Often these scheduling complexities surprise brides and grooms. Once you schedule the rehearsal and wedding dates and times, call back about a week later to verify your reservation to ensure that no misunderstanding has occurred.

There are some two hundred or so Catholic dioceses in the United States. While they each require similar paperwork, they do not always use the same forms. Once in a while, a local parish may insist on using the forms of *their* diocese and will not accept the forms of another one. This becomes a concern when either of you or both of you live in a diocese different from where you will celebrate your wedding. Ask the priest with whom you work. Ordinarily you will use the Church paperwork from the diocese in which the wedding occurs.

If neither of you has been married before, and at least one of you is a baptized practicing Catholic, most of the time you will need the following ten pieces of Church paperwork:

1. *A Pre-nuptial Questionnaire*

The priest has this at the parish and he fills it out with each of you individually. The primary purpose of this questionnaire is to protect each of you, the bride and groom, to ensure that each of you is approaching your wedding with the same freedom to marry and with a common understanding of the nature and requirements of a Catholic marriage.

2. *A new baptismal certificate for the groom*

Call the parish where you were baptized. They will ask when you were baptized, approximately. If it was within months of your birth, simply tell them your birth date. The parish staff will look up the exact date in their registry and then fill out an official form, stamp it with the church seal, and mail it to you.

You cannot use a years-old certificate which your parents saved from the day when you were baptized. Why? Because whenever you celebrate a sacrament, the church where you were baptized is notified. If, when you obtain a *new* baptismal certificate within six months of your wedding, the priest observes a notation of a previous marriage, then the priest needs to inquire and to request other documentation, e.g., a death certificate, a decree of annulment, etc. Otherwise, the priest cannot proceed with a Catholic wedding.

You only need the *date* of the Baptism (and Confirmation)

if you plan to celebrate your wedding at the *same church* where you were baptized or confirmed.

3. *A new baptismal certificate for the bride*

4. *A confirmation certificate for the groom*

Obtain this the same way as described for the baptismal certificate. According to canon law, if you are not confirmed and it is not possible to celebrate this sacrament without serious inconvenience, you may still celebrate the Sacrament of Matrimony. While this is true, since one becomes a full member of the Catholic Church with Confirmation, the Church recommends you celebrate the sacrament of Confirmation soon.[1]

5. *A confirmation certificate for the bride*

6. *A card indicating completion of marriage preparation*

For the last several decades, Church leaders have asked Catholics to prepare for the first celebration of every sacrament, since we can always learn more about the faith.

This makes good sense *provided* the programs which the local churches offer remain high-quality. Few things make educated people more upset than requiring an unhelpful program that seems to be a waste of time and money. Those in charge of diocesan Pre-Cana Programs have been working hard to overcome past criticism of these programs as being uneven. If the presenters offer wise insights in imaginative ways, these programs help. It can be tough going, though, if either the content or the method of teaching are mediocre to poor.

Engaged Encounter or Discovery Weekends have been spoken of favorably by those who have attended them. This seems partly due to the structure of these programs, since the "controls" are mostly in the hands of the engaged couples themselves. The presenters only focus on an area of married life briefly, and then the engaged couple spends most of the time working on the material alone as a couple. As long as you, the bride and groom, are willing to invest in quality reflection by yourself and in frank discussion with each other, then such preparation can be very helpful. Even if there is considerable diversity in the group as a whole, the two of you need to be on the same page.

Register as soon as possible for your marriage preparation program. In fact, it is recommended that you register for a program months ahead of time, if you can. Some of these fill to capacity quickly. Call the parish where you pray and request a listing of marriage preparation programs offered in the area in the coming months.

7. & 8. *Two witness affidavits for the groom*

Ask any two people who know you, the groom, well. These can be parents, friends, relatives—and they do not need to be Catholic. At present a priest or a deacon needs to fill out the affidavit with each witness. Usually it takes only ten minutes. The priest has access to these forms. Either ask your witness to call a nearby Catholic church and schedule a brief appointment or, if they worship at Sunday Mass, they could ask the priest after Mass if they could get together for a few minutes to complete the form to be a witness for their friend's wedding.

9. & 10. *Two witness affidavits for the bride*

Two additional people need to witness for the bride—different from the two for the groom. So, *four witnesses* in all are required. The primary purpose of these two witnesses for the bride and two for the groom is to protect you. It can help to have at least a few people besides the two of you to testify to your freedom to marry. These people who know you well will be asked to declare, to the best of their knowledge, that no extenuating circumstances exist which compromise the Catholic understanding of your faithful love commitment. Obviously, not everyone understands marriage the same way. Sometimes the differences are substantial and can, therefore, call the marriage into question.

A Catholic would ordinarily marry another Catholic. Why? Because you share with your spouse not only your house, your bank account, your body, but also your faith and the values which come from your faith. While this may be the case ordinarily and ideally, nonetheless God *truly* blesses us at times with relationships that do not fit our squeaky-clean categories. In this case, the Catholic party and the other than Catholic party need to understand marriage the same way to have a Catholic wedding. In such cases, the *Catholic* party needs to sit down with a priest and let him complete an additional form called a *dispensation.* Basically this is a way to formalize a legitimate exception. It includes a reaffirmation of the Catholic party's faith in Jesus within the Catholic tradition and a promise to do all in your power to share that faith with the children by having them baptized and raised in the faith.

Regarding the site of the wedding, you could choose to celebrate your wedding in a Catholic church with a Catholic priest presiding and the clergy of the other tradition could co-officiate. The presider (the primary leader) of the wedding is the one in whose house of worship you celebrate your wedding. Both the State and the Church insist that it needs to be clear that only one person presides over the rite of marriage (that is, the "*I do's*"). Other parts can be shared: readings, preaching, blessing prayers, etc. What also needs to remain clear, however, is that the clergy are there to serve you—and not the other way around. It is only natural and right that the clergy will want to present and focus and prioritize the concerns of their particular religious tradition regarding your wedding. This will be part of their service to you both.

You could also celebrate the wedding in a house of worship representative of your fiance's non-Catholic faith.[2] In such a case the Catholic priest can co-officiate if you want; but this is not required since, from a Catholic perspective, the minister of the sacrament is the bride to the groom and vice versa.

Paperwork can become a vehicle for you as bride and groom to experience further that this marriage is really happening! While compiling and completing the necessary forms, it is fairly common for the bride and groom to find their palms clammy at times, their stomachs and shoulders tight, their nerves a little on edge, and their faces a bit flushed on the brink of the magnitude of it all. This life commitment of love evokes a sense of awe and wonder—and sometimes fear and doubt and worry. The stakes are high. Reflect and pray alone and with each other, talk to one another so that you keep sorting out what is happening within you and your partner, especially what it all means to each of you. Offer support and let yourself be supported. Challenge one another. God and others will be there for you *if* you let them. This process of paperwork could well stir some of the best and the worst of your individual lives and your growing common life.

Summary Points:

* There are two kinds of paperwork: (1) State and (2) Church paperwork.
* The State marriage license must come *from the county in which you celebrate your wedding* in order to be valid.

* The State license is valid only for a specified number of days.
* By the time of the wedding rehearsal (at the latest), give the priest the State marriage license.
* A common mistake: reserving the reception hall just assuming that the church is available for *both* the rehearsal and the wedding.
* If neither of you has been married before and at least one of you practices the Catholic faith, you will likely need ten pieces of Church paper work:

    1. Prenuptial Questionnaire
    2. A new baptismal certificate for the groom
    3. A new baptismal certificate for the bride
    4. A confirmation certificate for the groom
    5. A confirmation certificate for the bride
    6. A card from the marriage preparation program
    7. Witness affidavit for the groom
    8. Witness affidavit for the groom
    9. Witness affidavit for the bride
    10. Witness affidavit for the bride

* If one of you is other than Catholic, the Catholic party needs a dispensation for a Catholic wedding.
* A joint ceremony is possible in any place of worship.
* Compiling and completing the necessary paperwork can stir a sense of awe and wonder—and sometimes frustration, fear, doubt, and worry. Offer one another support. Challenge one another to be the best you can be.

Notes

[1] Canon 1065 in *Code of Canon Law: Latin-English Edition* (Washington, DC: Canon Law Society of America, 1983), p. 389.

[2] You will need a dispensation from form for this. Your Catholic priest will help you with this.

Chapter Four

Options

> Assuming they had arrived at the office well-prepared to plan their wedding, within the first half hour of the planning, the bride and groom remarked with astonishment: "We had no idea how little we knew about the possibilities for creating our wedding."

A Catholic wedding contains a number of basic structural elements. Yet within this structure, you can choose from numerous possibilities. These choices will tailor the ceremony to the two of you and those who gather to celebrate with you.

Every Mass contains two principal parts: (1) The Liturgy of the Word (the Bible readings and the preaching), and (2) The Liturgy of the Eucharist (the table rituals Jesus left us, including Communion). At a wedding Mass, the Marriage Rite occurs between these two basic elements. These three parts form the central and most important part of the wedding Mass. In addition to these three central portions, there are subsidiary parts which flank them at the beginning and end of the liturgy. These are: (1) the Introductory Rites which help worshipers enter into the liturgy and (2) the Concluding Rites which help worshipers make the transition out of the liturgy and back to ordinary life. In summary, there are five parts to the wedding Mass:

I. Introductory Rites

II. Liturgy of the Word

III. Rite of Marriage

IV. Liturgy of the Eucharist

V. Closing Rites

I. Introductory Rites

The *introductory rites* gather people and prepare them to hear God's Word in this wedding context and to celebrate God's presence.[1] At a wedding liturgy, these rites usually include all or some of the following elements:

- Greeting and seating of guests
- Ceremonial Seating (grandparents, mothers, etc.)
- Entrance of the Wedding Party
- Call to Worship
- Opening Prayer

Gathering is not as simple a task as one might think, since individuals can be distracted, splintered, or preoccupied. What elements and structures will best help worshipers recollect themselves, and be fully present to what is taking place in the church? Also, what elements and structure will help the individuals sense that the gathering is a real community and not just individuals who happen to be together in the same place?

There are many ways to structure the entry of all the worshipers for your wedding. Think about options. Make choices carefully, because your decisions will establish a tone for the ceremony. Also, ask the priest to instruct those who will take a lead about specific details. For example, if you choose to have ushers, the priest will need to tell the ushers who is to be seated, where, and when.

Options for the General Seating of Guests

Some people choose to have ushers separate from groomsmen. In this case, the ushers alone would escort guests to their seats. The groomsmen would not assist in this task. Others choose to use some groomsmen to assist the ushers, especially if you plan a large wedding (over 100 guests). Generally you need at least one usher for every 50 guests at church.

You could have no ushers, no reserved seating for anyone, and the two of you could simply welcome your guests at the front door of the church.[2] This arrangement sets the tone for the beginning of your wedding in a way quite different from having ushers escort guests to specific rows in the church. At the very least, I would suggest that you reserve a front pew for your parents, or they could well feel discounted.

Such an alternative may seem like a radical departure from tradition. But, in point of fact, most of the numerous wedding options are not ancient. They are called "traditional," but usually this means they are common in the memories of those who live today. Often the roots of these memories are less than several generations past.[3]

Code language exists in the wedding situation. For example, it is "traditional" (living memory) to say to an usher when arriving at a wedding: "Hello, I am a friend of the bride." This statement intends to communicate a desire for the usher to escort the individual to the left side of the church (as one is facing the altar). (The groom's side is the right side.) In this option, the usher offers his left arm to the female guest, and he escorts her to the pews on the appropriate side. If the female guest arrived with her own male escort, he simply follows behind the usher and his female friend.

In recent years some have used female ushers, as well as male. If you choose this variation, the female usher usually does not offer her left arm to male guests with the female companion following behind them. Rather, the female usher simply walks side-by-side with the male guest, the female companion following behind them to the appropriate pew.

More often than not, if this kind of reserved seating is chosen, many brides and grooms will also set aside a handful of pews on the left for the bride's immediate family and on the right for the groom's immediate family. The bride and groom will inform immediate family members who are to be escorted to these pews that they are to simply tell the usher that they are part of the immediate family and are to be seated in a specific numbered pew on the left or right.

An option which eliminates one side of the church being noticeably fuller than the other and ensures that worshipers get as close to the central, primary actions as possible, is to have the ushers seat guests in whatever available pews are closest to the altar. The ushers should communicate to the guests that this arrangement is your expressed wish as bride and groom. However, *if* the guest contests and says: "I really want to sit on the bride's side," then the usher should of course comply. It is not a contest of wills. It is a chance to communicate a preference of the bride and groom.

Sometimes in addition to reserving front pews for the immediate family, couples reserve the first pew on the left for the women in the wedding party and the first pew on the right for the men in the wedding party. At other times, there is room near the altar for enough chairs to accommodate the entire wedding party, hence eliminating the need for them to sit in pews apart from the bride and groom.

You need to respect the rhythms and patterns of the local church community, without being straight-jacketed by them. It is not appropriate to barge inside a church and proceed carelessly, without regard for local custom. Some church staffs will have problems with seating all of the wedding party in the sanctuary. They will balk at such an idea and explain that this option is not allowed for a variety of reasons. These might include: "This area of the church is a sanctuary and sacred in character," or "We don't have enough chairs," or "There isn't enough room for all the chairs." Not a few times brides and grooms have offered to rent chairs and demonstrate that they can "make do" with a somewhat cozy arrangement for the wedding party in the sanctuary. If the parish staff refuses to allow this option, you must decide how important this consideration is to you. Enough to reconsider your choice of this church for your wedding?

Music will often accompany the seating of guests and ushers need to know if this is true, so that they do not *hold* guests until a song is finished. Also, ushers need to know where the restrooms are since they are the ones most likely to receive questions about their location.

You must also choose among options regarding a *runner*, a white cloth or paper which is unrolled down the center aisle. Some couples choose to eliminate it altogether. They do so for several reasons: (1) expense, (2) safety, potential for embarrassment. First of all, the florist supplies the runner, and usually for a cost. The church does not require a runner. Secondly, with the wedding party moving up and down the center aisle and the procession of gifts (bread and wine) and Communion procession also using it, the runner rarely remains flat. It folds and gathers in places (or sometimes rips if it is paper) and people can easily slip or trip on it.

To avoid the latter, the runner is often pulled down the aisle after the guests are seated, immediately before the procession of the wedding party. This arrangement is also rife with potential problems. Sometimes the runner gets stuck on one end of the roller. If the ushers are not looking back carefully and unroll it too quickly, the runner can break loose from the head of the aisle (near the altar); then, someone has to walk back up the center aisle and hold it with one foot, while the other continues to get the runner unrolled the rest of the way. Moreover, positioning the runner so that it is in the center of the aisle is easier said than done. More than a few beet-red ushers have tried to repair their well-intentioned efforts once they unrolled the runner three-quarters of the way down the aisle. The simplest, safest, and cheapest solution is to eliminate the runner.

But for a variety of motives, some couples really do want a runner. In this case, another option is to ask *your florist* to unroll the runner down the center aisle well before the guests arrive, when their staff brings the wedding flowers. Ask them to tie off the center aisle for the procession with a piece of white ribbon which can be easily removed for any ceremonial seating of the bride's and groom's parents and the procession of the wedding party. In this way, you can ask the florist to put double-stick tape under the runner every five feet or so (if there is stone or linoleum surface) or use decorative pins (if the aisle is carpeted). If you both choose this option, ask the priest to instruct the ushers during the rehearsal to escort worshipers to their seats via the *side* aisles, and let the guests move in to the center from there.

Would you like ceremonial seating, that is, the escorting up the center aisle (with a runner or not) of a few special guests? For example, you could invite particular ushers to escort a grandparent or godparents or a special aunt and uncle. If parents of the bride and groom are not processing with their son or daughter, usually the parents of the groom and then the bride are ceremonially seated last, just before the entrance of the wedding party.

If you want ceremonial seating for a few special guests, these can line up with their escorts immediately before the procession of the wedding party. Sometimes a special song is selected for the ceremonial seating. Sometimes the regular seating music simply continues so as not to complicate the Introductory Rites further. The musicians need to know if you want a special song and someone needs to cue them if there is a specific shift in music.

Options for the Entrance of the Wedding Party

Option 1:
TRADITIONAL ENTRANCE

The "traditional way" (living memory) is to have the men in the wedding party enter from the front right (facing the altar) and stand single file in front of the first right pew. The bride and groom determine the order of the men. Usually the groom is the last one to enter and the best man is second last. Before these two men, couples use any number of criteria to choose the order. Some examples include personal dynamics—who probably will get along well with whom; height (tallest to shortest or the opposite); or immediacy (family members first and friends later or vice versa). Still another thing that some couples consider is when different individuals entered your lives—newest to oldest friends or the reverse. As you can imagine, there is no one way to choose for everyone, every time, everywhere.

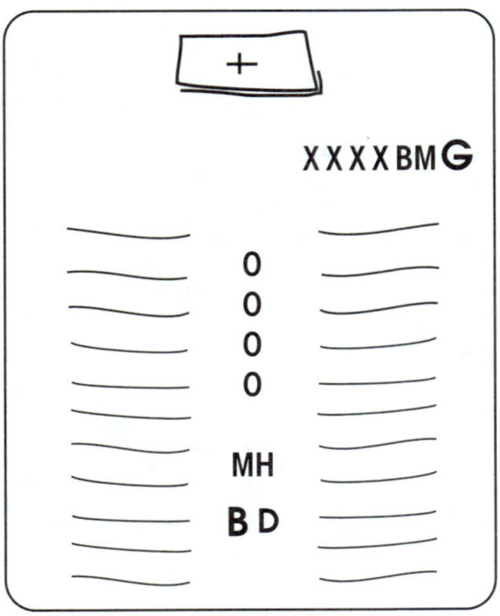

Option 2:
ENTRANCE IN COUPLES

In this time of increased gender sensitivity, some brides and grooms choose to have their wedding party enter as couples. Frequently individuals express relief at knowing they have a companion as they walk up the central aisle—rather than having to negotiate it all alone.

Option 3:
ENTRANCE USING TWO AISLES

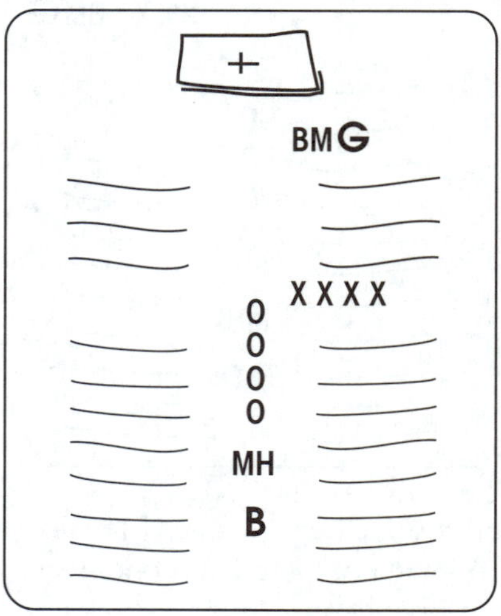

If there is a break in the middle of the pews on the right, some couples choose to have the women in the wedding party enter up the center aisle and meet their male escort halfway up the center aisle. In this case, sometimes the bride and groom will still ask the best man and groom to enter from the front right, stand before the first right pew, and meet the bride there.

Option 4:
ALTERNATE USE OF CENTER AISLE

Sometimes the groom will enter up the center aisle with the priest, followed by the couples, the maid of honor and best man, any children (ring bearer, flower girls), then the bride with her dad.

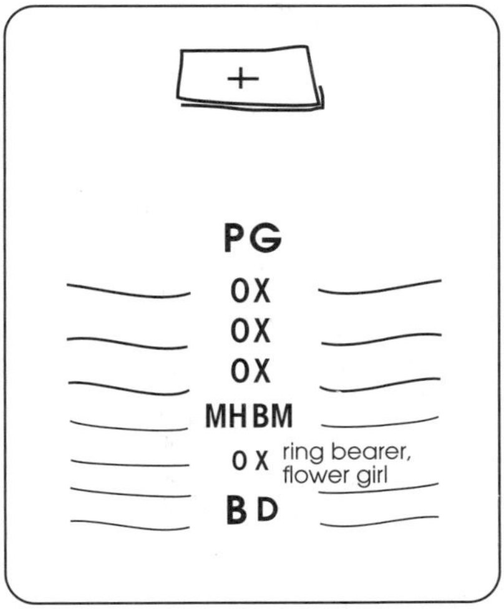

Option 5:
RE-ORDERED USE OF CENTER AISLE

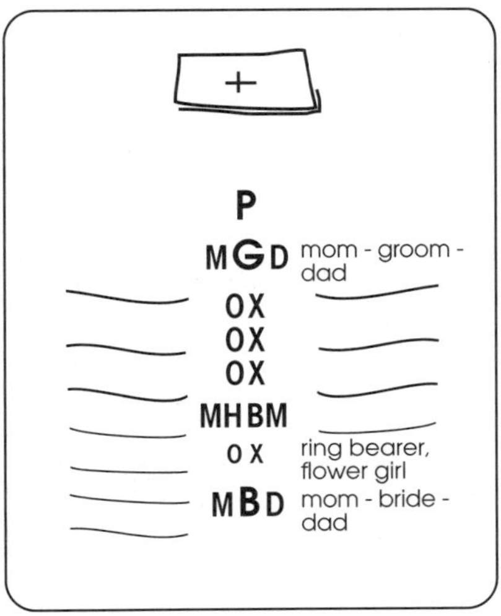

Sometimes the priest will process up the aisle first, followed immediately after by the groom with his mom and dad, then the couples in the wedding party, the kids, and finally the bride with her mom and dad.

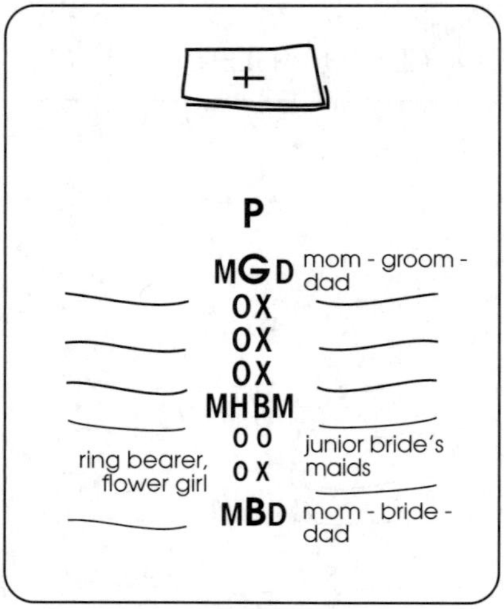

Option 6: LOCATION OF JUNIOR BRIDESMAIDS

If you choose junior bridesmaids, they would normally precede the children in the wedding party.

Option 7: WITH LIGHTING OF UNITY CANDLE

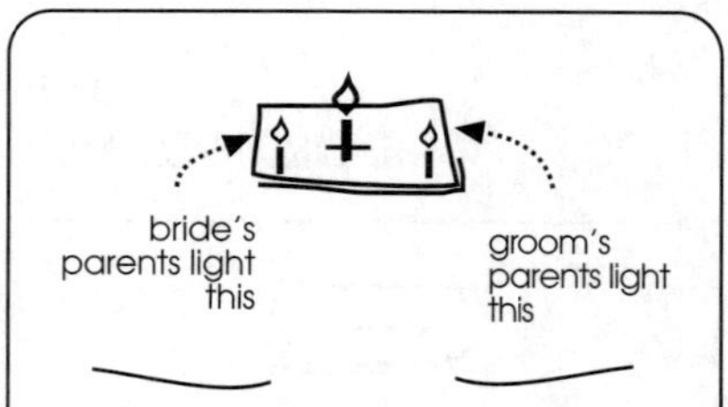

If you both opt for the use of a Unity Candle (a ritual lighting of a large single white candle near the altar during the Marriage Rite), you could ask the presider to tell the parents of the groom at the rehearsal to light the right smaller candle after they process up the center aisle, and then be seated in their pew, or return to the center aisle if they were escorting their son, the groom. In which case, the bride's parents could do the same with the left smaller candle. The father of the bride could either be seated or return to the center aisle if he was escorting his daughter, with or without his wife.

Option 8:
BRIDE AND GROOM PROCESS TOGETHER

The bride and groom could process together. Your parents (as couples) could immediately precede you in the procession, with the wedding party entering first.

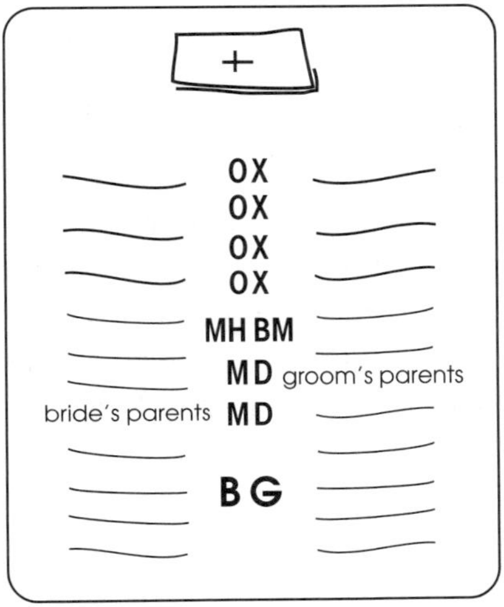

A variation on this theme would be to invite your parents to be escorted to their seats in the first pew right (groom's parents) and left (bride's parents), and then to invite your wedding party to enter with the two of you as bride and groom last.

These are the most frequent options. The list is not exhaustive. There may be others the two of you want to design. Feel free to create and to discuss the matter with the priest. The one request which seems to work best: let the priest lead the procession from the back of the church. Even with a wedding rehearsal the night before, invariably someone panics and needs some last-minute point of clarification.

Note well: ask your wedding party not to drink alcohol before the rehearsal and at the wedding ceremony itself. It is sad to say, but this protocol is no longer self-evident. Stories abound about someone in a wedding party demonstrating loud and obnoxious behavior after drinking. Alcohol at church is never appropriate, neither immediately before arriving at church for the rehearsal nor at the wedding itself.

One of the most significant choices you will make as a couple is how to arrange yourselves and your wedding party at the altar. This choice influences not only your experience as a marrying couple, but also the experience of all those in the church. For example, if you choose to kneel on a *prie-dieu* (kneeler) as soon as you reach the altar area, most of the time your family and friends will only see your back. They may well feel as if they are watching a ceremony between the two of you and the priest. Another way to express more clearly that the two of you celebrate the wedding and that you want the entire assembly to participate is to have the two of you turn around. Face the assembly as soon as you arrive at the altar. For example, you could create this arrangement:

	altar	
women in wedding party	*priest, bride & groom*	men in wedding party
bride's family		groom's family
guests		guests

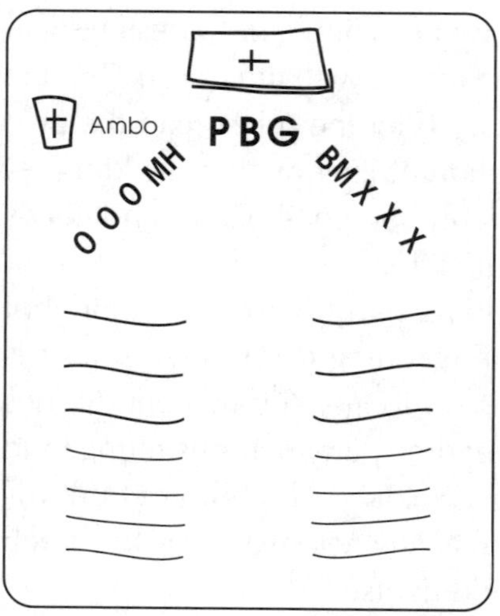

The opening rites conclude with the Opening Prayer. At the conclusion of this prayer, the priest invites the assembly to sit and to hear the Word of God. At this point, all the wedding party could sit too. If there is room, all could sit in the altar area. If not, the priest and the bride and groom could sit together, perhaps with the best man and best woman.[4] The rest of the wedding party could sit in the first pew on the left (women) and on the right (men).

II. The Liturgy of the Word

Most of the time, the readings from the Bible at a Catholic wedding Mass have this structure:

Old Testament reading
  Responsorial Psalm
New Testament reading
  Response of silence
  Gospel acclamation
Gospel reading
  Preaching (homily)

It is important to respect the dynamic of proclamation-response in the Liturgy of the Word. Notice in the structure how a response from the congregation follows the readings about what God has done for us. Often the Psalm Response is sung, among other reasons, to complement all the spoken words with another medium. This musical way of responding to what Christians call the Old Testament (also called the Hebrew Scriptures) originated in the Jewish roots of Christian worship.

The reform of the liturgy after the Second Vatican Council encouraged a recovery of the oldest tradition, namely, full, conscious, active participation of all the assembly.[5] As bride and groom, you yourselves embody this fundamental role by choosing both the Bible readings themselves (including the Gospel) and who will read the Old and New Testament passages. Especially if the church is spacious, choose readers who have the gift of proclamation, that is, those who can proclaim meaning in ways that can be readily understood by those assembled. It would also help if you carefully choose some women for leadership roles in your wedding.

The Catholic Church indicates the following options for scriptural texts at a Catholic wedding (*Partners in Life and Love,*

Alba House, and *Together for Life,* Ave Maria, have forms that can be filled out indicating to the priest your preferences for the options described here and elsewhere for your wedding Mass):

Old Testament Readings

Genesis 1:26-28, 31a
Genesis 2:18-24
Genesis 24:48-51, 58-67
Tobit 7:9-10, 11-15
Tobit 8:5-10
Song of Songs 2:8-10, 14, 16a; 8:6-7a
Ecclesiasticus 26:1-4, 16-21
Jeremiah 31:31-32a, 33-34a

New Testament Readings

Romans 8:31b-35, 37-39
Romans 12:1-2, 9-18 or Romans 12:1-2, 9-13
1 Corinthians 6:13c-15a, 17-20
1 Corinthians 12:31; 13:8a
Ephesians 5:2a, 21-33
Colossians 3:12-17
1 Peter 3:1-9
1 John 3:18-24
1 John 4:7-12
Revelation 19:1, 5-9a

Gospel Readings

Matthew 5:1-12
Matthew 5:13-16
Matthew 7:21, 24-29 or Matthew 7:21, 24-25
Matthew 19:3-6
Matthew 22:35-40

Mark 10:6-9
John 2:1-11
John 15:9-12
John 15:12-16
John 17:20-26 or John 17:20-23[6]

The customary proclaimer (reader) of the Gospel is a deacon. If one is not present, then another ordained priest (other than the presider) would do so. Only if there is no deacon and no other priest, would the presider proclaim the Gospel.[7]

Suggest a couple of ways the preacher could apply the proclaimed Scriptures to the lives of all who have assembled for your wedding, since this is the purpose of a homily.[8] The preacher will end the homily with a clear transition statement which indicates to all present that the two of you will now celebrate your marriage.

III. The Rite of Marriage

The basic structure of this rite is simple:

(1) Three questions (intention)
(2) Exchange of wedding vows (consent)
(3) Exchange of wedding rings

You could add (4) Unity Candle and (5) General Intercessions, but these last two are not required.

You should note that the Catholic Marriage Rite is being reconsidered. At this point it seems likely that the American Catholic Church may include additional options which have worked satisfactorily in other countries. For example, the relocation of the special blessing over the bride and groom (Nuptial Blessing) to immediately follow the vows may also be offered as an option in this country as it already is for those in Germany,[9] for example.

Arranging yourselves for this Rite of Marriage sends signals. You communicate meanings about your role and the role of the rest of the assembly.

Option #1

The two of you as bride and groom stand on an angle, so you can face each other when speaking to one another and also face the assembly and presider, who could be in the center aisle, near the front pews. The wedding party could then stand next to each of you on either side.

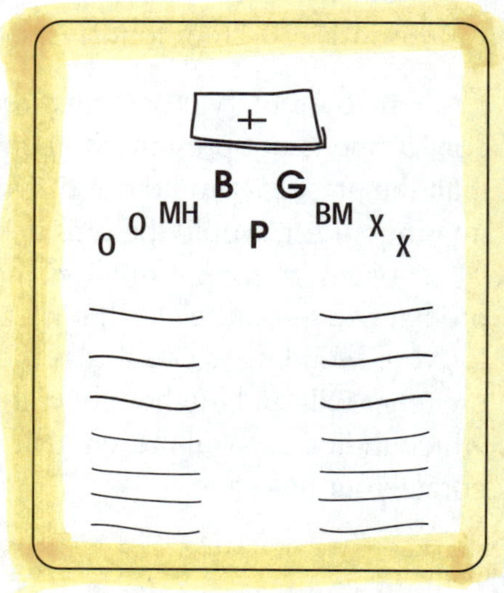

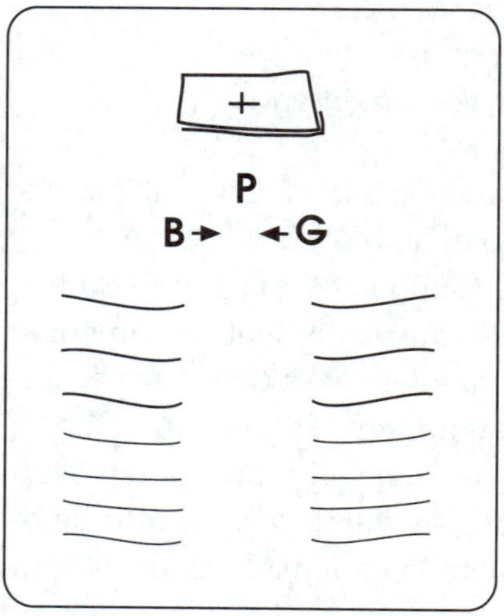

Option #2

The two of you face each other only, with the priest between you and the altar.

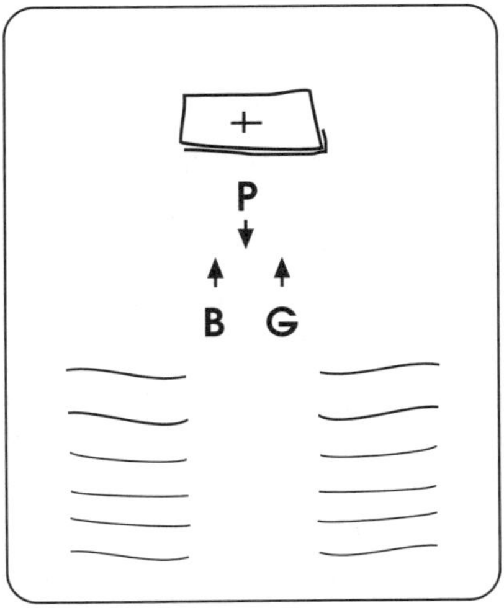

Option #3

The two of you face toward the priest only, with your backs toward everyone in the assembly. This arrangement tends to exclude most people in the church and leaves them feeling distant from the central actions, watching something take place in which they have little or no role. This arrangement does not foster full, conscious, active participation of all the assembly. Therefore, option #1 or #2 are preferable.

Questions

Three questions are asked in the Catholic Marriage Rite. In the months of preparation for your ceremony, you will talk about them with those who help you prepare for your wedding. This ritual asking of questions takes place in the context of a public prayer. Question #1 asks each of you to affirm publicly that you have come to the wedding freely and without reservations. Question #2 asks each of you to affirm publicly that you will love and honor each other as husband and wife for the rest of your lives. Question #3 asks each of you to affirm publicly that you will accept children lovingly, and raise them according to the law of Christ and the law of the Church, namely, love. These three questions express the Catholic understanding of the sacrament of marriage. Each of you needs to answer affirmatively and to vocalize your answer.

The Marriage Vows

After a brief introduction by the presider, the two of you can decide to pronounce your vows (marry each other) in one of the three following ways: (1) simply say "I do," or (2) repeat short phrases after the priest, or (3) memorize the vow formula. While currently there are two approved vow formulas, most couples prefer the newer version which continues to promise faithful love but does not use the words, *until death do us part.*

Some parishes will allow you to write your own vows provided they embody the Church's understanding of the sacrament. It is not a Catholic understanding to say: "I promise to give this marriage a good shot... or as long as it is mutually satisfying... or as long as we like each other, etc." Even if you are allowed to and choose to create your own vows, it is best that the presider have a copy so that if either of you draws a blank during the ceremony due to the intensity of emotions (this happens often) the presider can prompt you. If there is any hesitancy about using the wedding vow formula which you composed, ask the presider if he could allow your composition and supplement it (conclude your vows) with the approved formula. For example, after the groom vows his life to the bride, the presider could simply say to him: "And so, you do take (name) to be your wife and promise to be true to her in good times and in bad, in sickness and in health, and to love her and honor her all the days of your life?" The groom could answer simply: "I do." This may be a compromise which will satisfy both you and the requirements of the Church.

The Nuptial Blessing

In the name of the whole Church, the presider leads this special blessing of the newly married couple. As mentioned earlier, this prayer currently fits during the Communion Rite, later in the Mass. In Germany, this blessing follows the vows and replaces the presider's statement that the bride and groom have just declared their consent to this marriage. It seems more appropriate to ask God to bless the covenant which the two of you have just made at this point. If you were to use the Nuptial Blessing here, then you would omit it later in the Communion Rite, so as not to duplicate it. In addition, the whole wedding ceremony works better in terms of ritual movement if you place the Nuptial Blessing after the vows and if the presider is willing to do so. This modification seems minimally daring since Catholic bishops in other parts of the world have already approved it, and since it seems that it will become an approved alternative in the USA shortly. But technically, legally, this re-location is not yet approved in this country for Catholic weddings and the priest who will be presiding at your wedding may not allow it.

The Rings

If you have a young child as ring bearer, generally he or she carries plastic rings on a pillow—not the real rings. There are three important reasons for this: (1) The child may toss the pillow around and play with it, as children do, when someone is not looking. Horror stories abound about rings flying off the pillow. Someone may even know they are in the church *some place*; but the wedding is already fifteen minutes late. You could find yourselves borrowing wedding rings from others in the church, and looking for your rings later, after the ceremony. (2) There are other stories about the rings being tied onto the pillow so well that no one can untie the knot during the actual ceremony. Usually the assembly cannot decipher the cause for this delay in the ceremony. Then the assembly gets nervous or giddy as it becomes obvious they are trying to find someone with a knife or a pair of scissors to cut the ribbon. Rarely do worshipers attend a wedding carrying these instruments. (3) Children can "melt down" at any point. Most couples who want to include little ones think it is worth the gamble to let the kids walk up the aisle in the entrance procession and then slide into a pew toward the front with their family. Parents or grandparents should be alert to grab them if they get confused, and they can remain there in the pew throughout the wedding. Most recommend that either the best man keep both rings (the "traditional" approach, i.e., living memory) or that the best man keep the bride's ring and the best woman keep the groom's ring.

After the wedding vows (and maybe the Nuptial Blessing) whoever has the rings presents them. If you have altar servers, they can hold a dish to receive the rings. The priest prays a blessing prayer over them. Afterwards, the groom places the ring on his bride's hand up to the knuckle and speaks a brief line: ("[Name], take this ring as a sign of my love and fidelity"), concluding with the words of the Sign of the Cross, "in the name of the Father, and of the Son, and of the Holy Spirit." The bride then slides the ring on the rest of the way. There are two reasons for letting the bride slide the ring onto her finger the rest of the way. One reason is symbolic, another pragmatic. The symbolic reason: someone may want to offer you a gift; but if you are unwilling to receive it, the gift is going nowhere. By putting on the ring the rest of the way, you are saying in effect: (a) "I accept your gift of yourself," (b) "I want this relationship," (c) "I am glad to receive you as my spouse," (d) "I am proud to wear this ring and to have you as my spouse," etc. The pragmatic reason: sometimes when you are excited, your fingers swell. Even though the ring was fitted to your hand, it may not slide easily past your knuckle at the actual ceremony. Rather than try to maintain a pleasant look on your face while your spouse tries to force the ring, you can simply let the ring be wedged there at your knuckle for the time being. A couple of hours later, once your feelings settle down, it will probably fit well.

The Unity Candle

This item continues to stir controversy in the Church. Ironically, thoughtful Catholic people *divide* over the use of the Unity Candle. For one reason, some say the meaning of this ritual lighting seems unclear.[10] For example, does it signify that the two lives are now one? Or, does it signify in a ritualized way that the two of you are one *in Christ*? The bride's and groom's individual candles are extinguished, but surely it is not true that individuality is snuffed out in a Christian marriage. Is this candle lighting merely a Hallmark moment of trendy emotionalism? Others say the power of symbol lies in its triggering many meanings at once. They would hold that American assemblies are sophisticated enough to know that whatever meaning is attached to this ceremony, it should not distract from the practical Catholic understanding of the union effected by marriage.

Perhaps some larger issues exist with regard to the Candle. For example, the entire liturgy can become too wordy. The ritual cries for vehicles to express and to cultivate Christian meanings in ways other than words.

Another concern is that the altar is not a utility table. Unfortunately, some couples place the Unity Candle on the altar. Catholic directives state clearly that only the bread, wine, and presider's book should rest on the altar itself.[11]

Give all these thoughts some consideration, perhaps read a little on the matter, and then after talking over the issue together, decide if you want a Unity Candle. If you do, usually you will need to purchase one along with the two tapers you each use to light it. You could spend less than ten dollars on one; but you could also spend more than a hundred. For merchants, weddings are a business.

The General Intercessions

Sometimes Catholics refer to these as Prayers of the Faithful. These prayers address the needs of the world, the larger Church, and the local community gathered at the wedding, obviously including the bride and groom. In practice, sometimes these prayers get focused exclusively on the bride and groom. It is better to consider not only yourselves and those gathered for the wedding, but also others in the world and the larger Church.

Like the Unity Candle, the General Intercessions are optional. Sometimes brides and grooms want to offer an explicit prayer for relatives who have died, for others in the assembly who celebrate wedding anniversaries, for all married couples present, etc. A different approach would be to pray for the dead during the Eucharistic Prayer, and refer to the anniversaries and other married people during the preaching. Another option would be to pray for all these concerns during a *meditation* which you as bride and groom could compose. One of your friends or family could read this *after Communion,* provided you do not choose other rituals at this point.

IV. The Liturgy of the Eucharist

Presentation of the Gifts
Prayer Over the Gifts
Nuptial Preface
  Holy
Eucharistic Prayer
  Memorial Acclamation
  Amen
Lord's Prayer
  Nuptial Blessing (if it was not done after the vows)
  Peace Rite
  Fraction Rite
Communion
  Prayer After Communion

After the Liturgy of the Word and the Marriage Rite, this is the third major section of the wedding Mass. It follows the exchange of rings or the lighting of the Unity Candle or the General Intercessions—depending upon how you choose to conclude the Marriage Rite. One non-verbal way to communicate this shift in ritual is for the entire wedding party to gather around the altar with the priest. They could all simply form a semi-circle around the altar, the assembly on one side, and you, the priest and the wedding party on the other.

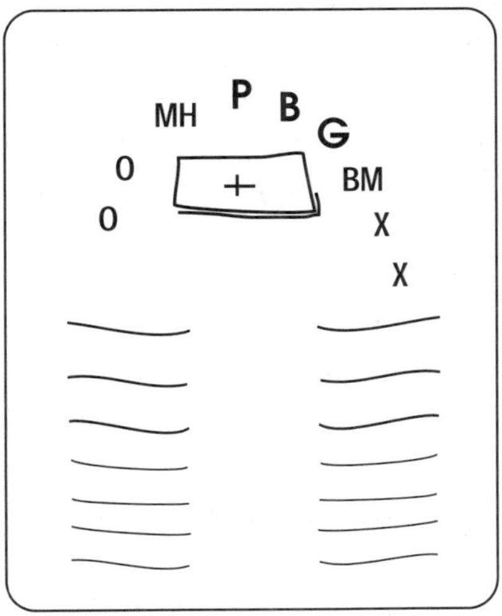

Since it is preferable to broaden participation of others in the assembly, you might want to invite someone to bake the bread for your wedding Eucharist, rather than simply use hosts from the parish. Besides, the Catholic Church recommends we use bread that looks and tastes more like food.[12] Most of the time, people are honored to be invited to help you in this way. Someone can bake the bread a week or two before the wedding and freeze it. They can bring it to the rehearsal frozen. (See Appendix A for an easy recipe.) If you know a wine maker, you could invite him or her to bring the wine. You could invite those who baked the bread and made the wine to process them to the altar. Another option would be to invite godparents or other family members and friends to bring up the bread and wine at the Presentation of the Gifts.

After the priest receives the bread and wine, in silence he will ritually present the gifts (dramatically show them) to the entire assembly while the music continues. This is called the Presentation of the Gifts. The presider will then speak the Prayer Over the Gifts and begin a Nuptial Preface, a special matrimonial beginning of the Eucharistic Prayer (the thanksgiving prayer over the bread and wine). Within this section of the Mass, there are three Eucharistic acclamations: (1) the "Holy," (2) the Memorial Acclamation, "Christ has died...," and (3) the "Amen."

After the Eucharistic Prayer, the assembly prays the Lord's Prayer. The presider then leads the Nuptial Blessing, if this was not prayed already after the wedding vows. Next comes the Greeting of Peace. Some brides and grooms like to present their parents with flowers at this point in their wedding. Often the mothers already have a corsage and to juggle more flowers at this juncture seems cumbersome and redundant. But some still want to use this symbolic gesture of presenting flowers. In which case, inform your florist what you need. Invite your maid of honor to hand these flowers to the two of you, after you kiss each other and greet the priest, when you make your move toward your parents in the front pews.

A caution: without realizing it, you can prolong the exchange of peace beyond what is helpful to the whole assembly. As bride and groom, you know most of the people in church and will likely be drawn to each person whose eyes you see. Often it will not be easy to bring this Peace Rite to an end.

A suggestion: aim to limit your greeting to the priest, your parents, and the members of your wedding party.

After the Greeting of Peace, the Fraction Rite occurs. Another helpful way to include others in liturgical leadership roles is to invite two people to help distribute Communion. While everyone is greeting one another during the Rite of Peace, a few trained Eucharistic Ministers can come forward to the altar to assist in the breaking of the Eucharistic bread and the pouring of the Eucharistic wine. Before presenting Communion to the assembly, you might consider asking if the priest will address a few words to those who cannot receive Communion. You may well have guests of other religions or those for whom it would be inappropriate to receive Communion because they are not in full communion with God and the Church. For example, the presider could say: "For those who would like to receive Communion… (then give traffic patterns); and for those who will not receive Communion, for whatever reason, if you would like to receive an individual blessing instead, simply come forward in the same line. When you reach the head of the aisle, bow your head and I will rest my hand on your shoulder and offer a brief blessing prayer."[13] Once you and the wedding party receive Communion or a blessing, the presider and Eucharistic Ministers will distribute Communion or a blessing to the entire assembly. You and the wedding party could sit, rest, and pray while Communion continues.

After Communion, some couples choose a procession to Mary's statue with a small bouquet of flowers. In the recent past, the bride alone went to Mary's statue, sometimes accompanied by her maid of honor or mother. More often now, if couples include this ritual, they go together as husband and wife. This is not a required ritual for a Catholic wedding. More and more couples choose not to include it within the wedding itself for a variety of reasons. Some have a devotion to Mary, but prefer to express this private devotion earlier in the week rather than in public with everyone watching and with little participation by the entire assembly. Some do not have a particular devotion to Mary, so it does not seem authentic and integral for them. Some prefer another kind of meditation after Communion. This can take a musical or prose form, and can be composed by the bride and groom. (See Appendix B for several examples.) And finally, the presider leads the Prayer After Communion to conclude the Liturgy of the Eucharist.

V. The Concluding Rites

Greeting
Blessing
Dismissal or Ritual Introduction
Recessional
Postlude

The presider begins this section with a ritual greeting: "The Lord be with you." He then leads a blessing prayer over all the assembly. This can take several forms—from the longer and more solemn to the shorter and more simple. Many couples prefer the last option given all that has preceded in the ceremony.

After the blessing, some couples prefer a usual dismissal rite, "The (Wedding) Mass is ended, go in peace to love and serve the Lord." Often they prefer this because they abhor clapping in church. They want a more formal tone to end the ceremony. Another possibility would be a ritual introduction of the two of you as husband and wife. Two issues to consider are:

(1) How would you like the presider to introduce you? Options include:

> "Mr. and Mrs. William Smith"
> "Mr. and Mrs. William and Mary Smith"
> "Bill and Mary Smith"
> "Bill and Mary Jones-Smith"

(2) Most in the USA will applaud if the priest formally introduces you. Many enjoy the applause. At this point, you could kiss again, the bride could receive her flowers back from the best woman, and then lead the recession from the altar.

Usually a recessional accompanies the exit of the newly married couple, the best man and woman, and the rest of the wedding party. For the most part, it is the reverse order of the entrance procession, the women in the wedding party taking the right arm of the men before recessing down the center aisle. Instrumental music (a postlude) can accompany the exit of all the worshipers.

It helps photographers if you ask the wedding party and whomever else you want in photos (parents? grandparents? altar servers? readers?) to talk with friends later at the reception. Ask them to follow the two of you down the center aisle and back to the altar area for photographs.

To summarize, then, you could encourage family and friends to participate more fully, consciously, and actively in your Wedding Mass in a variety of ways. The following list of options presents some of them.

* to help prepare an order of service (program)
* to prepare the environment for worship (flowers, liturgical hangings, etc.)
* to participate in the wedding party
* to usher by welcoming guests and escorting them to seats
* to play musical instruments
* to sing
* to bake bread
* to make wine
* to distribute orders of service at the back of the aisles
* to bring up the gifts of bread and wine
* to read: an Old Testament reading, a New Testament reading, or possibly a Meditation after Communion
* to distribute Communion
* to serve at the altar (altar servers)

Some cultures include additional roles. For example, the Hispanic and Filipino traditions include a *madrina* and a *padrino* for coins, lasso, etc.

Notes

[1] The "General Instruction of the Roman Missal" in *The Sacramentary* (New York: Catholic Book Publishing Company, 1985), number 24.

[2] If you choose this option, be prepared to face at least two possible scenarios: (1) a range of reactions from guests, including those who think a bride should never see her groom before the altar on the day of the wedding; (2) guests tend to arrive at the last minute, and if you meet them at the doors, they will want to chat for a while. Starting the ceremony close to "on time" then becomes a problem. Since multiple ceremonies are frequently scheduled close to one another at a church, you may need to sacrifice pictures at the conclusion of your wedding because it started later than you had planned.

[3] See "Union" by Robert Fulghum in *From Beginning to End: The Rituals of Our Lives* (New York: Ballantine Books, 1996), p. 117 ff.

[4] Sometimes the term you use matters more than you might think initially. *Maid of honor* traditionally referred to the unmarried female who is closest to the bride. *Matron of honor* was used for one who was married. Some people do not want to be called a maid or matron of any kind. In which case, *best woman* has emerged as the term of choice.

[5] *The Constitution on the Sacred Liturgy,* number 14.

[6] The International Commission on English in the Liturgy, *The Rites of the Catholic Church* (New York: Pueblo Publishing Company, 1976), pp. 558-561.

[7] "The General Instruction of the Roman Missal," number 34. Also see Congregation of Rites, instruction *Inter oecumenici,* number 50.

[8] "The General Instruction of the Roman Missal," number 41. Also see *Inter oecumenici,* number 54.

[9] German Martinez, "The Newly Revised Roman Rite for Celebrating Marriage," *Worship,* 69 (March 1995), 136.

[10] Paul Covino, "Customs Quaint and Curious: Making Good Choices," *Assembly* 18 (July 1992), 568-569.

[11] Bishops' Committee on the Liturgy, *Environment and Art in Catholic Worship* (Washington, DC: United States Catholic Conference, 1978), number 88.

[12] "General Instruction of the Roman Missal," number 283.

[13] This prayer should be simple and constructed in such a way that a person who believed in God from any tradition would feel included. For example: "May you know that God is with you, especially in times of trouble."

Chapter Five

What About the Music?

> If two or more trained conscientious church musicians get together and they work for the Catholic Church, they invariably play a game called "I've Got a Better One." The conversation goes like this:
>
> "Did you hear about the parish where a man dressed up like Santa Claus and led the procession for Mid-night Mass?"
>
> "I've got a better one: Don't forget the weddings. There was the case of '*Goin' to the Chapel*' (a hit by the Dixie Cups) being used as a wedding processional. Sometimes the music that couples pick for their wedding could be used later as grounds for an annulment."[1]

In retrospect, the wedding stories that are told at a session of "I've Got a Better One" seem humorous and entertaining, but when they actually happen, they are more often than not a source of frustration and even anger for those who are preparing their wedding liturgy as well as for the musician(s) they've asked to help. Couples deal with many new details and professionals as they plan, but they are often least familiar with what's involved in selecting music, contracting musicians, and having them perform so as to foster and enable the prayer of the people assembled in church.

The goal of this chapter is to help you do that. We'll begin with some general principles that liturgical musicians use to plan music for various kinds of worship services, and then we'll look at specific options and details in terms of the actual musicians and music for a wedding.

The foremost principle that everyone involved in planning the music must consider is that *the music must be at the service of prayer*. Just as we saw in chapter one, it is your wedding, but the ritual also belongs to those who assemble with you. If you have thought about making your wedding liturgy your own, you no doubt have some ideas about the music in both general and specific terms. This is highly desirable, but you must remember to weigh those choices and ideas against the fact that the music must first be prayerful. It can be elegant, stylish, jubilant, or boisterous, but no matter what style or character you choose, the music must first be able to foster and sustain the full, active, and conscious participation of your guests.

Music of any style can do this if it is chosen carefully. The first consideration is that a piece of music shouldn't divert attention from the prayer. This is especially true for music that is sung. A good planning principle is that any music that is sung within the liturgy should have a scriptural text or be based on a paraphrase of Scripture. There are exceptions to this, especially when the text itself is a prayer (for example, Leonard Bernstein's "One Hand, One Heart" from *West Side Story*), but for the most part, music with non-scriptural texts (show tunes, popular ballads) belongs outside the service itself, possibly used for gathering music in the opening rites or as your celebration continues at the reception.

A second important consideration is that the music used within the wedding should be familiar to those assembled. You and the musician(s) in charge need to learn what music is most familiar to the people who gather there for worship on a weekly basis. If your wedding is at a parish or church that isn't home to either of you, you should help your musicians formulate an idea of what your assembled guests are used to from their various worship experiences. Experienced and competent church musicians will ask you about this; if they don't, be sure to let them know that it's important to you and that you would like them to plan accordingly.

Having thought along these lines as a couple, you will next want to contact a musician as early as possible. Like priests, caterers, florists, and banquet halls, musicians are often booked months, if not years, in advance. You may already have someone in mind to do the music. If not, you can ask your presider for some contacts, call the director of music at your home parish, or even the liturgy office of your local diocese. In your selection process, be sure that the lead musician is not only a competent performer, but also has experience with liturgical music. This is crucial for the overall timing, pace, and prayerfulness of the celebration. Also consider putting one musician in charge of everything else, including contracting additional singers and instrumentalists that you may want, planning rehearsals, and making any other necessary musical arrangements. Having a single person in charge will facilitate communication and avoid having "too many cooks ruin the soup."

If you know the local parish musicians to be competent, you should strongly consider hiring them. They have the advantage of familiarity and experience with the local environment and people. On the other hand, you may have a close friend or know of another competent musician from your worship in other places. If you choose someone from outside the church where the wedding will occur, be sure to clear this with that church. In some places you may be asked to pay a fee even if you don't use the parish musicians. This is because the base salary of a parish musician is often supplemented on a contractual basis with stipends from weddings and funerals. In other places, a significant investment has been made in instruments like pianos and pipe organs, and the parish is not anxious to risk damage and abuse to the instruments from total strangers. As we've seen in earlier chapters, planning ahead is the best way to anticipate and work with all the unknown factors.

When you have contracted the services of the lead musician, you should present your initial ideas to him or her, perhaps by telephone. At this point, you need to focus on the other musicians that you will want to be present so that additional contracting can occur early. This is one of the services that you'll want the lead musician to take care of, unless you already have specific players or singers in mind. The lead musician will typically have a number of reliable players that he or she has worked with. This makes everything function more smoothly. If you have additional people that you wish to be involved, provide the lead musician with a means to get in touch with them and leave the arrangements to the musician in charge. Remember, the communication should occur between the musician in charge and the other musicians. You do not want to be in the middle, or you may find yourself dealing with matters that are beyond your competence.

A minimum number of players for a wedding liturgy is probably two. One musician will normally function as a keyboard accompanist and should typically play piano or organ. A second key player would be a singer who has experience as a cantor. This individual must go beyond solo singing and understand how to involve the assembly with sung prayer. These two people will be able to execute all of the various kinds of music that are required, including solos (for instance the processional and recessional marches or vocal selections as your guests are being seated) as well as lead the service music such

Chapter Six

The High Cost of Marrying

> In a moment of honesty, the bride braved the candid comment: "I've just always imagined my wedding this way. I don't care what it costs. I'm going for it."

This wedding that you have always imagined—is it worth it at *all* costs? From what has preceded this chapter, it is clear that there are many ways to look at your wedding. For example, you can look at it from the vantage point of the *time* and *energy* you invest in celebrating this eventful juncture in your life. You can consider it from the angle of each family member. There are *emotional benefits* for each and *emotional costs* for each, albeit usually hidden from immediate view. Examining various perspectives enables you to formulate the question in a more personal way: Is this kind of wedding worth it *for us*? Surely a Christian couple needs to take care that they do not get so caught up in the wedding ceremony that they forget their married life.

The costs are more than financial, though they certainly include these. In the spring of 1998, CNN Headline News reported $20,000.00 to be the average cost of an American wedding. A recent broadcast on a Chicago radio station stated the average cost for a wedding with 200 guests in New York was $29,400.00 and in Chicago was $19,100.00.[1] Whatever the specific amount, it is often sizable.

Some would say this amount of money is outrageous, especially for a Christian who claims to have faith which prioritizes values beyond how things look, feel, taste, smell, and sound. And yet, even these deeper truths can be expressed and cultivated through the media of the senses. However you look at it, these choices about how much to spend and in what ways deserve careful consideration.

Most people enjoy a good celebration. What makes one celebration better than another depends upon the individual making the judgment and the underlying criteria for the judgment. For example, some would say the volume and the quality of the alcohol is the ultimate criterion. Others would say that attention to the details of the wedding, e.g., the beauty of the dress, the prayerfulness of the wedding ceremony, the variety and uniqueness of the flowers, the lavishness of the food and drink, the quality of the music, how many dance with abandon, etc., are good barometers of the success of the wedding. How will you assess the quality of your wedding celebration?

Is there a financial ceiling you want to or need to maintain as you make your choices about how to celebrate this event in your life? The amount of money you and your families have will affect your choices. There are limits for all people—financial and otherwise. Unfortunately, in this country not a few have taken out large loans and gone deeply into debt for many years to finance this one celebration. Do not attempt to "keep up with the Joneses," even if they only live in your imagination. Deal with your exaggerated notions. Another way to proceed would be to simplify the expectations of your wedding. For example, some couples choose not to register at major department stores for gifts, but instead invite guests to offer whatever amount of money they like to help them work toward a down-payment on their first home. Of course, some are put-off by such a request since they have never heard of such a thing and they find it crass.

Others think it emphasizes the needs of the marrying couple more, which seems more to the point if indeed the wedding is for the bride and groom.

Amazingly, Americans will usually expect to pay thousands of dollars for the wedding rehearsal dinner and wedding reception, and yet feel misgivings about offering the church a few hundred. Perhaps it is due to a predisposition that the church should operate on grace alone. But, truth be told, there are bills for heating, electricity, cleaning, repairs, etc.

Jokes abound regarding the periodic abuses of money and power in the Church. Marriage preparation programs are not "money makers" for the Catholic Church. If as bride and groom you cannot afford the published costs of a program you think would serve you best, ask if the parish or diocese has a sliding scale. Ask if you could pay in installments. Most will accommodate.

Summary Points:

* The costs are more than financial—and for more than the bride and groom.
* Determine your budget based on your Christian values and your means.
* Consider the amount you contribute to the church compared to reception halls.
* Ask for special payment plans if needed, for the sake of being better prepared for your married *life*.

Notes

[1] On 12 May 1998, WMAQ Radio Station quoted "Bride Magazine" as the source for their statistics.

Appendix A

Recipes for Eucharistic Bread

Recipe 1

2/3 cup unbleached white flour
1/3 cup whole wheat flour
1/2 cup sparkling water (such as Perrier, the bubbles aid in baking the interior of the loaf in the absence of leaven)

1. Preheat oven to 400°F. Spray a 9-inch pie plate with cooking spray (such as Pam) and wipe off the excess.
2. Mix the ingredients in cold bowl. Add more water if necessary to form a ball. Flatten the dough into the pie plate and score into 100 or so pieces.
3. Bake for 15 minutes. Prick the top with a fork, turn loaf over, and bake 5 more minutes. Turn over again and bake 5 more minutes.
4. Cool on a wire rack. Wrap tightly and store in a plastic bag. It is best to offer the bread fresh, but it may be frozen for future use.

Recipe 2

2 1/2 cups whole wheat flour
1/2 cup unbleached flour
1 1/4 cups lukewarm water

Mix all the ingredients together in a bowl until all the flour is gathered together. Knead for 6 to 8 minutes.

Shape into two 8-inch rounds. Roll the dough to a disk about 1/4 inch thick and place on greased cookie sheet.

Bake immediately in a 350° oven for 16-17 minutes. The color will lighten somewhat. Take care not to over bake.

Cool and wrap in plastic or foil until ready to use. May be frozen.

Appendix B

More Resources for Music

Handbook of Music for Church Weddings, by Mary Beth Kunde-Anderson and David Anderson. Liturgy Training Publications, Chicago, IL.

> Though this was written for musicians who work with couples as they prepare the liturgy for their wedding, you could benefit from it as well. The listing of specific music is especially helpful.

The Bride's Guide to Wedding Music. Ariocombe, Mariner; Toulouse Chamber Orchestra and the Academy of St. Martin in the Field, Angel #64899. One compact disc.

> Mainly instrumental music with a wide variety of ensembles. Useful for broadening your choice of options and finding the titles of music that might be familiar to you. Most of the orchestra pieces exist in standard keyboard reductions.

The Bride's Guide to Wedding Music, vol 2. English Chamber Orchestra, Westchester Cathedral Choir, Angel #66817. One compact disc.

> Similar to volume 1, but with slightly more music meant to be sung.

Sound the Trumpet, English Ceremonial Music for Trumpet, Organ, and Percussion. Edward Carroll (trumpet) and William Neil (organ). Newport Classics, #60038. One compact disc.

Excellent for getting to know some of the many options for processional and recessional marches.

ST PAULS

This book was designed and published by St. Pauls/ Alba House, the publishing arm of the Society of St. Paul, an international religious congregation of priests and brothers dedicated to serving the Church through the communications media. For information regarding this and associated ministries of the Pauline Family of Congregations, write to the Vocation Director, Society of St. Paul, 7050 Pinehurst, Dearborn, Michigan 48126. Phone (313) 582-3798 or check our internet site, www.albahouse.org